Denied Love

Denied Love

By:
Clarence Kittrell

XULON PRESS

Xulon Press
2301 Lucien Way #415
Maitland, FL 32751
407.339.4217
www.xulonpress.com

Unless otherwise indicated, Scripture quotations taken
from the King James Version (KJV) – *public domain*.

Printed in the United States of America.

ISBN-13: 978-1-6312-9152-4

Acknowledgements

1st, I would like to Thank my Lord and
Savior Jesus Christ who is everything to me.
I would like to thank Kristi Wright for transcribing
my recording into words. She is a life saver. Also,
I would like to thank my brother Apostle Victor Hick
for editing it for me. Last my Family and the whole
True Vine family for the support.

I love you all and God Bless you.

Apostle Clarence Kittrell

Table of Contents:

PREFACE

THE NAME OF THE BOOK IS *DENIED LOVE*. THIS book literally will change your life. I encourage you to read all of it in its entirety; I promise you, you'll understand by the end. The one thing about this book is it talks about a past, a present, and a future. And, in this book, your past can affect your future and your present, but once you realize in your present that "my life is going in a circle" the change must come.

Chapter 1: The Beginning

A LONG TIME AGO, THERE WAS A MAN NAMED James and a woman named Martha. Martha chased James all over the place. She was very fond of him. James was very active in sports. James was quite the athlete and was always playing some type of sports. He was a boxer, played football, and played basketball. Even though Martha was very fond of him, James was a player. He continued to play his games, and his mind was not settled for Martha.

Martha continued to pursue James. Although James had relationships with other women Martha was determined to be with James. With that in mind she looked beyond James' other relationships and she waited for him to be her own. Martha was a good student in school. Yet, her attention was focused more on matters of the heart than academics. Her main priority at that point was him and she continued to follow James. At some point James began to realize that she was determined to be with him. They began a romantic relationship at some point during the year Martha graduated from high school. One day they were together after one of James' basketball games. This was just after Martha had graduated from high school. Martha had been a good student in school and she was planning on going to college. However, her life plans were drastically changed when during that summer she found out that she was pregnant with James' baby. They were living in a very small town and with her parents. During this period of history it was common that when an unwed woman became pregnant that the father of the child was expected to marry the woman. This tradition of a man marrying a woman whom he got pregnant was considered "the right thing to do." James, however was not very happy to be pressured into marrying Martha just because she was pregnant. He was very upset about marrying Martha because he saw an unwanted marriage and the responsibility of raising a child was going to limit his chanced of living the life he imagined. He was young and athletic and wanted to enjoy a carefree existence. He did not want to be tied down. He wanted to travel and experience life on his terms. James believe that this situation would essentially put an end to all his plans.

Against his own personal wishes, James conformed to the social norms of the day and decided to marry Martha. Even though James was high-spirited and Martha had low self-esteem, they continued to live together, but they decided to move away from the small town they lived in. They moved north to a town called Muncie, Indiana. Here, they lived with their aunt.

James began to settle down and found a job that his uncle helped him to find. Martha grew in her pregnancy. One day, the babe was born a little girl. Her name was Crystal. Crystal was stillborn. The loss of their firstborn child was devastating for the young couple. Yet, in the midst of this turmoil they continued to press through this challenging and heartbreaking time in their lives. The journey of their lives together things continued to evolve.

Following their tragic loss, Martha decided to enroll in nursing school to become a registered nurse. As she went through school, she began working in a hospital.

A year-and-a-half later, Martha became pregnant again. This pregnancy was normal and Martha gave birth to a healthy baby girl. They named the little girl Karen and gave her the nickname of "KK."

As Karen grew up, everybody was very fond of her from James's family. So much so, that it bothered Martha because they paid no attention to her, but they paid much attention to the baby. James told her that it was her imagination and to stop worrying about it. But, she knew that something was wrong, so they got their own place.

They started living as a family, and they worked, hiring babysitters to care for the children. Suddenly, something happened, again. This was the time that was going to change their lives. Martha was pregnant again.

Martha really wasn't ready for this pregnancy, and James was very upset because he had not planned on having another child so quickly. Martha's aunt said to him, "It takes two to tango," so James just dealt with it.

The one thing about this baby forming inside of Martha was that, from the moment Martha found out that she was pregnant, she was always getting sick. She had no idea what was going on with her. As the baby was growing, she noticed that the activity of this baby was remarkable. The child would not be still. Even the doctors were astonished that this child moved so much inside of her.

Because she was going to school, she loved to read. For some reason, though, when she was almost finished with her degree, she took on more classes. This time, she took Bible classes. Because of these classes, she was reading the Bible more, and she noticed that every time she looked up James was out with his friends, always at the bar. She was getting really, really upset about it. So, the only thing that she knew to do was what told her aunt told her to do, "pray."

The baby inside of her just would not be still. She would always talk to him, but that baby just kept kicking and moving. One day she picked up her Bible, and she had no idea where to start reading. So, she began in the book of Genesis. She noticed that every time she would read the Bible, the baby would always keep still. Martha saw that is appeared that when she would read the scriptures aloud it was if the baby was sitting there listening.

4

After she would finish her reading, the baby would turn over and rest. She couldn't understand why this was happening. Martha ignored it, and she continued to read. She read all the way from the book of Genesis through Exodus. These Bible study sessions seemed to increase the connection between mother and son. She seemed to intuitively know what the child needed in terms of food and rest. When she read the scripture the mother and child dynamic increased on a major level. It was as though the baby was already formed inside of her and had been born how he was inside of her.

When Martha next went to the doctor to have a check-up, she told the doctor about this development. The doctor said it was really abnormal for a baby inside of her at six months to be doing these things. They then told her to keep them posted on the activity of the baby.

Martha continued to read, but she noticed something. By the time she got to Deuteronomy, there was something happening. She started having dreams. As she was dreaming, it was as if she could see her baby. Martha had no idea what was happening, but it was as if someone was telling her about him, about this babe that was on the inside of her, or about what was going to happen.

Martha told James about it, and James kind of laughed at her saying, "Yeah right." He went out and about his way, and Martha got a little upset with him because she felt he wasn't listening to her.

He would always play with the baby Karen. Martha was getting jealous because he was forgetting about her. As time went on and her due date grew near, she kept telling James that he needed to stay around because she was getting closer and closer to having the baby. James said, "Don't worry. I'll be there, I'll be there, stop worrying me. Let me go out and have fun with my friends." Martha cried. She was very upset, and she prayed for him.

Suddenly, it was as if the baby told her to pick up the Bible because he became very feisty. As she started talking to him and rubbing her stomach she said, "Baby, it will be okay. Baby, it will be okay." Martha started reading to him. The baby settled and started listening. By the time she got to the Book of Revelation, she didn't understand what was going on with the baby. This one time, he was really moving still. As she got toward the end of Revelation, she couldn't understand what was going on. She said, "Why is he kicking my stomach so hard? I thought that reading would keep him still." She had reached her nine months but thought that she would have at least two or three more weeks, but he kept kicking.

One day as she was having something to eat, she was reading to him. She got to the last chapter of the book of Revelation, and all of a sudden, her water broke.

Chapter 2: The Journey

THE WATER BROKE, SO THE EXCITEMENT started. Martha got on the phone and called her aunt. "Have you seen James?"

Her aunt told her, "No." Martha was getting really upset, and her aunt asked her what was going on?

"My water broke," she said.

Her aunt said, "Well if you can't do anything, call a cab."

Martha was upset because there was a snowstorm outside. "The cab won't be able to get to me. Let me look make a few phone calls to see if I can find James."

She found James quickly, and he rushed to the house. He got in the car, and they began to drive. They were sliding all over the place, so he got behind a slow a snowplow, and he followed the snow plow all the way to the hospital. He told her, "Hold on hold on don't have that baby in my car."

As Martha was looking at him, she said, "I'm about to have the baby; I can't help it." Martha was really upset because he was worried more about his car than he was about her having the baby. They made it to the hospital just in time. Immediately, they rushed her into the delivery room. Seconds later a baby was born!

There was something different about this baby. James did not like this baby because this baby was not the same complexion of him. It wasn't the same complexion as their daughter Karen. James even questioned if the baby was his, and Martha exclaimed, "Of course it's yours! I can't even believe that you would even say anything like this to me."

And he said , "Okay," so she named their son James Jr.

James Jr. looked at her, and she said to him, "You have cost me a lot of things. I don't know what your life is going to be like, but understand Mommy will always be here for you." Martha had no idea about this baby that was born. So, she continued to stay in the hospital for a few days, and then they brought James Junior home.

They quickly noticed that Karen did not like her little brother. Little Karen was not getting the attention that she was used to getting. So, little Karen hit her brother. Martha told her that was not nice and that she must not hit him.

So Karen cried and ran to her father. And James took little Karen in his arms and told her, "Oh, you're not being neglected; you're being loved." But she didn't understand because she was still very young. This did not stop her from becoming jealous of her brother getting into things. Karen started acting out because she wanted attention from everyone.

Martha noticed James didn't want to pick up the baby. He didn't want to because in his mind, he still felt like something was wrong because the baby did not have the same complexion as him. James Sr. said, "I'm not crazy, I know something is wrong." But what James didn't understand was that Martha hadn't been with anyone else because she had to take off of work.

Little James Jr. had given her so much grief during her pregnancy. Martha continue to live through the things that she was living through and do the things that she was doing. She would breastfeed the baby. Every time it was time to eat, he was always ready to eat. She said, "He has strong appetite."

The doctor told Martha that the baby needed more than just breast milk for sustenance. So, they tried to give him different types of milk, but every milk that they tried was unsuitable for him. He would always get sick. She wondered what was going on with her baby. The doctors said they had no idea. They tried every type of formula for him, but James couldn't digest any of them properly. The baby's doctor said, "Well, I guess we have to go back to old school methods. Do all the things that we had to do before new things came about." So, they gave him goat's milk, and goat milk, was accepted.

James continued to grow and be well. He loved the goat's milk. He loved to eat and drink. The one thing that changed in Martha's life was that Martha would open her Bible in the middle of the night when the baby would not stop crying. She remembered when she was pregnant, he was feisty, but when she would start to read, he would stop moving. The baby would just be still. As Martha would read, James Jr. stopped crying, and he looked at her as if he was in a class. Martha said, "wow!" By the time she was at the end of a chapter, the boy would fall asleep. The only time he would get upset was if he was hungry or something. But when she opened the Bible to read to him, he would be quiet. Martha noticed James Sr. was getting closer to his daughter, but he didn't want anything to do with little James Jr.

Martha was very upset about that because she felt it wasn't right. She talked to her aunt about it, and they talked to James. But James ignored it. James said, "I don't think that this child is mine."

So, Martha decided, "It doesn't matter because I'm going to take care of this baby. This baby will have the greatest of love." Martha had no idea what she had just said.

The one thing about the baby was that, when he went to sleep, James Jr. would always be laughing in his sleep. "I don't understand why you keep laughing and moving," said Martha.

Her aunt told her, "I think you should call your mom."

She called her mom and asked her about it. Her mother told her, "The reason why the baby is laughing is because there are angels around him. They are entertaining the baby. "Honey, don't be upset about what this baby is doing. God has something special for him."

Martha listened to her mother and said, "I have no idea why when he's upset, I read him the Bible and he's just as quiet. And by the time I get to the end of a book of the Bible, he trips off into sleep."

Her mother said, "You have no idea what's about to happen in your life. He's going to change many people's lives. Martha, I know that I wasn't able to give you things in your life, and I know that hurt you, but I did the best I could."

Martha understood. She hung up the phone, and as soon as she saw that James Jr. was hungry, she fed him.

James Jr. grew stronger and stronger. Martha would say to him, "You're starting to get a little bigger; it's kind of hard to carry you around." Little James Jr. didn't crawl, he scooted. One day while he was in his baby bed, he pulled up on the bed, and he lifted himself. Martha looked over at James Jr. and said, "Are you trying to walk? Are you trying to get up?" As she picked him up, he smiled at her. She said, "Are you trying to walk?" He laughed. Martha said, "It's time to read," and the baby laughed again.

As she started to read, she set him down in his chair, but for some reason James Jr. didn't want any food. So, she just went on and read to him. As she was reading, he was quiet, but she had to stop because the phone rang. Now, he was hungry. He started to eat as she fed him while she was talking on the phone. When Martha got off the phone James Jr. didn't want any food. She gave him a bottle. He enjoyed it and fell off to sleep.

She got him a walker and put him in it. She noticed that his little legs were getting stronger. Her mother warned her that she needed to be careful with little boys, because they were very, very curious. Her mother also advised that to make sure he was safe, she should put things out of reach of James because he would touch everything once he started walking. So, Martha listened, but she soon forgot about it.

James Jr. learned how to walk. Martha said, "What am I going to do with you? Every time I look up, you're grabbing something off the table, and you're messing with the outlets." She laughed at him. She said, "I'm going to put him in the bassinet." Next thing she knew, he was climbing up out of the bassinet. So, she put it up a little higher, so he wouldn't be able to climb out of it.

James was laid off work, so Martha found a job. She went back to the hospital to continue working as a registered nurse. When she got home, she would fix dinner for James. He then got a new job factory.

James Sr. still would not pay any attention to little James Jr. Instead, Karen got all the attention. On their birthdays, grandmothers would send over some money. Five dollars would be sent to Karen, and James Jr. would receive a dollar. This bothered Martha because she wanted her children to be treated equally. "James Jr. don't worry; God is going to give you everything that someone is not giving you." Martha would tell him.

Martha talked to James about it. James said, "I can't give him money. Move on!" Martha was so upset about it.

Martha noticed that James Jr. had something different about him. One day, Martha went to his bedroom to tuck him in, and he hugged her and said, "Mommy it be okay, it be okay, love you."

She cried, and she said, "I love you too, baby." When James Jr. went to sleep, he'd laugh in his sleep.

Then there was another time when he went to sleep, and he felt someone tickling his feet. He said, "Mama, Mama, they're tickling my feet."

Martha said, "James Jr., go to sleep."

So, James just went to sleep. She knew that something was different, but she had no idea what was about to happen in this whole ordeal.

Chapter 3. Life Changing

JAMES JR. WAS A VERY, VERY CURIOUS YOUNG boy. As James Jr. turned three years old. Once, he reached into the fishbowl and pulled the fish out. No one even knew what happened to the fish. They had to assume James Jr. ate the fish. Another day Karen, James Sr., and Martha were looking for him all over the house. They kept calling for James Jr., but he was nowhere to be found. As they were looking around, James Sr. went to the refrigerator and to get something to drink, opened the door, and there he was, little James, at the bottom of the refrigerator in the chocolate cake. Everyone started to laugh, and Martha was very upset because she thought he could have suffocated in the refrigerator. "You guys are here, laughing? Do you have any idea what could have happened?" asked Martha. They thought that she was overreacting. This caused James to be watched much closer. They also noticed, not only was he curious, but he was extremely clumsy. He was always falling and pulling on things.

Every time James Jr. was going to sleep, something would happen which would cause him to pull the cover up over his head. Martha asked him one day what was wrong. James Jr. said, "When you leave out, they're running around my bed, and they tickle me."

She asked, "Who baby?"

"My friends," said James Jr.

And Martha said, "What friends?"

James Jr. tole, "The ones that are in my dream. They're here in this room."

Martha looked at him, but ignored him and laughed. She said, "Baby that's just your imagination."

He said, "No Mommy, they are here. They're like light, and they run around. They chased me in my dreams. We have a lot of fun."

Martha said, "You're probably dreaming about your sister Karen.

But he insisted, "No, Mommy, these are my angels."

She stopped and looked at him. Martha didn't say anything. She hugged him and told him to go to sleep. So, James Jr. went off to sleep, and the next day his mother got up for work.

As she was leaving from home, she went to see James and Junior off. She said, "Alright, I'm getting ready to go to work. See you guys later."

And James Jr. said, "Okay, Mom, love you."

Martha said, "I love you too baby."

So, Martha went off to work. Little James went back to sleep. The babysitter came over to watch the kids. The babysitter was one who would always be on the phone. If the kids needed something, she would go get it for them.

Little James would sit in the chair and eat his lunch, then he would go and play. He loved playing outside. One day, he was playing on his big wheel and little Karen was playing on her bike. The kids decided to trade. Karen gave him the bike, even though James didn't know how to ride the bike. Little James Jr. turned the bike over. He saw that the babysitter was looking, and she asked James to turn the bike back . She watched him do it and then walked away. James Jr. turned the bike back over again, not listening to her. He started spinning the bike wheel harder and harder, and he stuck his finger in the bicycle spoke. His finger cut off. Little Karen was screaming and crying because little James's finger was severed. When he looked at his finger, he passed out. Quickly, the babysitter hung up the phone and called 911. James's mother ran across the street to see what was going on once she got home, but the ambulance came.

They were looking for the finger and couldn't find it, so they patched him up and put him in the ambulance. James looked up as the paramedic was standing over him. When he looked up, he passed out again. The next time little James finally woke up, he was in the hospital, and his mom was standing over. It was the same hospital where she worked. His uncles and everyone were standing over him when he passed out again. A strange thing happened while he was in surgery that was life changing. James Jr. stayed asleep for two-and-a-half weeks. Doctors had no idea what had happened. Even though it was his little finger, he had lost a lot of blood. He went into shock and was out for two-and-a-half weeks.

His mom was sitting in the room praying for him, and she read the Bible to him during the time that he was out. James Sr. was nowhere to be found. Martha was really getting upset, because the child needed blood. Everyone was trying to give him blood, but they weren't the right match. But, the one thing that James found out when he finally came in was that this child was his. All the time he thought that this child was not his, but he had to give him blood.

Once James Jr. woke up, his mother and his father were there. They said, "We thought we were going to lose you, what happened?"

And he told his mother, "Mommy, I was looking at you guys. Every time that you cried, He told me to tell you, it's going to be okay."

Martha asked, "Who told you that James Jr.?"

"Michael."

And she said, "Michael who?"

"That's my angel, Mommy."

Startled, she stared at him. Then she said, "What else did he tell you?"

"He showed me the world. We walked around, and we're the same age, walking around. He was talking with me, and we were having fun in the sandbox. He told me it was time for me to go. Then I laid down on the bed, and I woke up and you guys were here."

So, when his father heard it, he looked at him, but didn't understand what was going on and why. He had so many questions in his mind. He thought his son was suffering from brain damage. Martha called her mother to find out what was going on with him. She told Martha that James Jr. was very, very special. He was more than she knew. Martha's mother said, "Reading the Bible had nothing to do with you, it had everything to do with him."

James Jr. continued to grow. He and his sister finally started going to school. Their parents put them in private schools. Little James Jr. and Karen had no idea why they were going to the private school. They wanted to go to the regular school with all the other kids, but James Sr. didn't want them to.

Little Karen wanted to go and play with everyone. Karen had a feisty spirit, and every time she went somewhere, she wanted to fight. She wanted to fight the little kids in school, and she wanted to fight the teacher. She wanted to do some of everything.

During the time that little James Jr. was in school, he kept looking down the hall to see who was coming. James Jr. could feel when his father was in the school. His father would bring them lunch. He asked the teacher if he could go to the restroom, and she let him go. He saw his dad walking down the hallway, and he shouted, "Dad!"

"What are you doing in this hallway?" His dad asked.

James said, "I don't know, I just knew you were coming here." James Sr. had no idea little James Jr. was so gifted.

When James Sr. looked in little Karen's room, she was sitting in the corner with her hair all over the place. He found that little Karen had an altercation with a teacher. So, James got her and took her in the bathroom, and he disciplined, then took her back into the class and made her apologize to the teacher in front of the class. He told her to sit down and don't do anything else.

Martha and James started having marital problems. They had no idea what was going in each other's lives. They eventually separated. James stayed in Indiana. Martha went back home to Illinois, where she stayed with her sister. The kids moved with her. She soon found a place of her own. She started working for Kohl's Department Store and stayed there for a very long time. The only thing that Martha was doing was selling shoes. During this time that she was working, the kids missed their father so badly. They would ask her about when were they going back home. Martha said, "We're going home in time." Whenever Martha went to go see her sister Louis, her sister loved Little James Jr. She favored him so very much. Anything that little man wanted, she gave him. She knew little James loved to eat. Every time he was hungry, she told him that she was his second mom, and whatever he wanted to eat, she gave it.

One day, his Uncle Watty, his Aunt Louis's husband, came home and asked, "You want to go fishing?" So, he took James Jr. fishing.

While he was out there on the boat with his Uncle Watty, James kept standing up. His uncle told James to stop standing up because he was going to fall in the water. As little James threw the fishing rod out into the water, he fell in the water. When he fell in, his uncle jumped in to save him and he brought James out of the water.

He said, "Son, I told you not to stand up."

Little James said, "But, I caught a fish."

His uncle told him, "I know, but you should have left it for me." He had cautioned James about catching the fish because he was not an experienced fisherman and needed his uncle's help to reel in the fish. He also knew that James was not used to being out on the water in a boat.

They went home and had a few fish, and James Jr. showed Aunt Louis that he caught a small fish. She fixed the fish for him, and he ate it.

One day, Aunt Louis and Martha had an argument. They were very upset with each other.

James Jr. cried, "I want to go home to my daddy." And, Martha just looked at him.

Louis told Martha, "I think you should take them home."

So, she got on the bus and took them back home to Indiana.

There was something different that Martha had to see when she got home. She found out James was saved. He was going to church and was clean. Every day, they went to church as a family. They went to Bible study, and they went to prayer meetings. In this church, there was a pastor whose name was Pastor Henry. One day, he walked up to him James Jr. who was now nine years old. He asked him if he was the son of James Sr.

James Jr. said, "Yes sir, I am."

The pastor said, "Let me ask you a question."

James said, "Yes sir."

"When are you going to preach, preacher?"

Little James looked at him and laughed. "What do you mean?" And then went on his way.

As time went on, James was in school, and things started to change in his life. His older sister never played with him. Karen was very feisty. Every time you looked up, Karen was in a fight with someone. Little James couldn't understand why.

When she wanted to go outside, she'd go and ask her mother Martha. Martha would say no. She would then go ask her father. He would ask Karen what her mom said, and Karen would say, "Mom said come and ask you."

James Sr. said, "Are you guys done with your chores?"

Karen said, "Yes, sir."

So, he said that they could go outside. Karen would go back inside and tell little James, "Dad said we can go outside." There was this back and forth about whether they could go outside and play. Karen started playing them against each other.

Soon James and his sister joined the choir. Their mother and father took over the junior choir, because the other director was becoming feeble and older. When they took over the choir, they went and picked up all the little kids. The choir was huge. Little James started singing. He did a solo. Everyone loved it. "He's going to be special." said the pastor.

One day after church service was over, James Jr. was on the way out the door when the pastor walked up to him and tapped him on the shoulder.

James Jr. turned around and looked up to him and said, "Sir."

The pastor asked, "What are you going to preach, preacher?"

Little James just laughed and walked away.

James later went home and took a nap. He had a dream. In his dream, someone told him, "It is time for you to be baptized, so that you can come even closer." James Jr. told his father that he had to be baptized.

His father asked him, "Why?"

"Because the Lord told me it's time," said James Jr.

The next Sunday, the pastor opened the doors of the church and started accepting people for baptism. James

Jr. was afraid to go upfront by himself, so he laid down on the pew. His father came around and pick him up. Little James broke out in tears.

The pastor said to the congregation, "I just came back from the Holy Land, and the Lord told me this young man is going to speak to the nations." The pastor started to praising God. He said that's the reason why he kept walking up to him.

The next Sunday, James Jr. got baptized. The pastor told him everything that was going to happen. When James went into the water, he noticed something different about himself. He could see and hear things that he had never seen or heard before. His life was changing.

Chapter 4.
Everything New

EXPERIENCING SO MANY NEW THINGS IN HIS young life, James Jr. knew that there was something different. Suddenly, James had fire to read his Bible, but he had no idea where to start. Although, he was going to Sunday school and Bibles study every Sunday, he had so many questions. He would ask the deacons who were teaching, but no one could answer the questions that he would ask. His father told him that while he was in class, he was supposed to listen and just hear what they had to say. James Jr. said, "I can't understand why they won't answer my question every time I ask." James Jr.'s dad told him to just listen and learn, and James told him he would.

While James Jr. was in school, he always wanted to do good. He also wanted to play with his sister, but she had no desire to play with him. She used to call little James "crazy" because he'd say, "You don't have to play with me, my friends will play with me." The whole time that James was in school, Karen would always get into fights. She would run to her little brother James and ask for help. James would always help his big sister no matter what, but then Karen would leave him by himself and play with her friends. As James was growing up, he tried to make friends. Other kids would bully him, mess with him, and would not want to be his friend. Little James would just find something else to do like walk around outside. He would just watch people play.

His first two years in high school, James liked a girl. He really, really liked her. And he started talking with her. He thought to himself, *she has the same spirit that I do*. Her name was Gina. He was very crazy about Gina; but suddenly, Gina's mom got sick, and they moved away. Little James was very hurt because Gina was the only friend that he had.

As time went on, James moved up in school. Little James loved to run. James Sr. put James Jr. and his sister in summer track and field. Little James was very short, but he still wanted to win. He kept running. He said one day he was going to win the race. His sister was very fast. He decided to run with the high school track team. He won one race. One boy teased him and said James only won the race because he was not running.

James Jr. Laughed at the boy and continued to ignore him. He told his dad that he wanted to play football. Martha said, "No, you're not out there to get hurt."

So, James Sr. said, "Let the boy play football. Let the boy play."

Little James was very short, like a little runt, just sitting out there on the bench. Everyone would get to play except for him. He would have on his shoulder pads, his shoes, and everything, but he would never get to go into the game. The coach finally tried him out on the kickoff team.

One day, someone got hurt so they put little James on the receiving team. He caught the ball effortlessly. They all looked at him catch as though he was a pro while he was running. He ran to the right; he ran to the left. He saw somebody was running after him, and he ran with all his might because he was so scared. He got a touchdown! His coach said to him, "Great job, Lil' James!" Little James earned a spot on the kickoff team. Every time there was a kickoff in the middle of the field, James was placed in the backfield.

Though he was short, he could catch the ball and run really fast, but he wanted to be better. He asked his dad to help him.

His dad asked, "What do you want me to do little James?"

And, he said, "Can you help me to get faster?"

James Sr. said, "You sure this is what you want me to do, little James?"

Little James said, "Yes, sir."

So, his dad took him to a park called Story Land Zoo, and it was full of hills. James Sr. said, "This is what I want you to do. Run every one of these hills."

Lil James asked, "Do you want me to run up and down the hills?"

James Sr. said, "No, turn and run up the hills, and you when you get back down the hill, I want you to run back up the hill."

Little James turn to his dad and said, "Dad, the hills are so steep. How am I going to make it to the top?"

James Sr. said, "I want you to run with all of your might to the top of these hills."

Little James had a determination. Because he was so close to the ground every time he was running up the steep hills, it was like he was crawling up the hills. He was very determined that he was going to get up the hills. Little James decided that he was going to do it, so he kept doing it and succeeded.

When it was time for the football game, he went to practice. His coach looked at him and said, "James Jr., run out there and keep running." He told the quarterback Chris to throw him the ball. Chris the quarterback threw him the pass and little James caught it.

One day during the kickoff return, their star receiver pulled a hamstring at the end of the game. Everyone told James Jr., "Coach Badge is calling you."

Little James went to his coach, "Yes, sir."

The coach said, "This is what I want you to do. I need you to run down the field in a straight line and turn around, then reach out and catch the ball. I need you to run down the field; don't turn, don't look anywhere else, just turn around, and catch the ball."

Little James said, "Okay!"

The coach gave him a count of three.

As there was ten seconds left in the game, Chris went back to pass. James took off running. He was running at the same speed as the ball, while Chris threw it down field. James Jr. turned around and caught the ball in the end zone for a touchdown. From that point on, James's life was forever changed. Suddenly, he went from the person that was no good, to the star player on the team. And, he was a star receiver at that. So, when he got to his tenth and eleventh grade years, he was catching passes no matter where they threw the ball. One time, he did a reverse catch. They tossed him the ball, while it was raining outside, and he cut down the field.

James Jr. remained humble about who he was and how good he was, but there was one little girl that he loved. He her name was Judy. He was crazy about Judy during the time they were in school. But Judy changed schools, and he was really upset about that. He continued to stay in touch with her.

There was something different that was happening in James's life, and Martha could notice it. Every time he came home, before he would do his homework, he would pray. He would pray when he got up in the morning. He would also pray when he was on the way to school while he was on the school bus. Karen would ask James Jr. if there was something wrong with him, because he'd be sitting there talking to himself while on the school bus. James Jr. would say, "Karen, I'm not talking to myself. I'm talking with someone." She never understood him.

One day during a game, James Jr. jumped up to catch a football, and a teammate jumped out on him. James broke his kneecap. Doctors told him that if he got hit in his knee again, he would never be able to walk. James Jr. was devastated. There were schools that were talking to him about playing college football. He felt like his life had ended.

Fortunately for James Jr., he was perfect in everything he did. Even in his schoolwork. He had a grade point average of 3.67. He almost got straight A's in high school. James Jr. graduated from high school, went to community college, and he found work. The college was right next to the Kroger's that he worked for as a bagger. Everything was about a competition with him. James was different. He went to the same college as Karen. James could not type like everyone else because his finger had been cut off. They put him on the electric typewriter, and he did very well.

James Jr. had become very close to his father in his teenage years. But, his father was very hard on him. He would tell him to stop playing around. To stop laughing. Take life seriously. He'd tell him that life was not a game. James Jr. understood his father. This made him strong. His father became his best friend.

One day, his father fell asleep while they were watching TV, so he got up and said, "I'm going to bed." Little James said good night, and James Sr. went to sleep. Even though Little James had his own room upstairs, he decided to remain on the couch downstairs. He had a very uneasy feeling. His father had made a noise after he went to sleep on the couch, and James Jr. couldn't figure out what was wrong with him.

The James Jr. heard his mother Martha say, "James, turn over!" She turned on the light and look at him. His eyes were opened, while he was making that noise. She cried "James! James!"

Instantly, Little James ran upstairs to see what was going on. He saw that his father was a shell. He was gone. Quickly, he got on top of his father and started giving him CPR. He had learned it in class. They called 911, and the police came and proceeded to administer CPR.

During the time paramedics were administering CPR, Martha was running all over the house saying, "What am I going to do? Where is he at? I'm losing my best friend." Paramedics tried to do all they could. They put Little James out of the room.

While he was pacing, his uncle came to him and said, "Son, I know this is hard for you. I'm going to be here for you. But the paramedics want to know what you guys want to do."

And James asked, "What do you mean?"

He said, "Your dad is just holding on with a little bit of life. They want to know if you want them to continue to resuscitate him."

Little James Jr. said, "I don't know. Continue to try."

They tried, but it was unsuccessful, so they stopped. James Jr. was heartbroken.

One day he went outside, stood on the porch and he looked up in the sky. He said, "My dad is gone. The only thing I have is You know. What else? Please don't leave me. Please don't leave me."

The family buried their father. Martha had a hard time dealing with her husband's death. Karen was a daddy's girl, so she was grieving. As Karen became an adult, she used the company of boyfriend to suppress every bit of pain she was having about her father's passing. Everyone turned to James Jr. to be the man of the house. He had no idea what to do. The only thing he knew was that he was going to work and go to school.

There was a lot going on in their home at the time. Frustrated by many of the issues they were facing at the time Lil James and his family did not always get along well. Filling in the role as the man of the house Lil James took more of a leading position. One day, while listening to Karen complain about her job Lil James told his sister that he would help her get her quit. Later, he signed for her to go to school. As time went on, Little James found himself getting caught up in a sort of rut in his life. He was going to school going to work, coming back home, and going to church. He found himself spiritually unfulfilled. His family asked why Lil James seemed to hate going to their church and did not enjoy attending church service anymore? He answered that he no longer was being spiritually fed in that ministry. He expressed his desire for more of God and the church no longer seemed to be helping him grow in Christ. Because the church I changed. He told Karen "I need more." Although she did not fully understand what he meant Lil James was determined to do deeper in God. He continued to express his desire for more of God and that the ministry they attended not enough for him. So James started visiting other churches looking for a new church home.

And she noticed something different about James. She felt like he was pulling away from her. One day James went to sleep and in his dreams the Lord said to him that he wanted him to go to a land he would show him. James enlisted in the Army. Ask him one day oh, and he told her. She said, "Why are you leaving?"

And he said, "Because the Lord told me that I must leave and go to a land where He will show me."

And she said okay, then little James left.

Chapter 5:
Beginning a Journey

LITTLE JAMES DECIDED TO GO INTO THE Army. As he was looking back over his life, he was remembering how he'd been denied and how he was not accepted by everyone. He was looking over those things and could understand what God was doing in his life. He was understanding why He was taking him from his family. He was concerned about his mother Martha, since it had been four years since his father had passed. During that time, he was with his friends, but he never had a chance to mourn, because he had to be strong for his mother and sister. His family turned to James Jr. to make decisions, even though he was only nineteen years old. James was very afraid because he had never been away from home before.

He had no idea what to do or what to say. He did not know what was right or was wrong. He would just try to make the best decisions that he knew how to make. When he began his military career, Little James was stationed in Fort Knox, Kentucky. He was in the resting area just before they came and got him for basic training. As he was sitting there, he saw four of the drill sergeants come in yelling and screaming. They were trying to get them up early to ready the recruits for what was to come. James got afraid.

After dinner, James called home. The sergeants had taken away everyone's phones so they couldn't talk to anyone. He made a collect call home to his mom and said, "Mom, I want to come back home."

She said, "No! The Lord told you to go there, and you stay there. I'm proud of you." You're going to make it! This is going to change your life forever." She said, "You're not little James anymore. Your father has passed. You're not James Jr. You're James now. I'm proud of you. I want you to make me proud of you. I want you to go in there and do everything God is telling you to do."

James went back to the barracks where he was staying, and the day came when they came to get him and all the other recruits that were there. They called them soldiers. As they got them all up out of the bed, they told them to get on the truck. They had gotten them uniforms and everything. When they got on the truck, they were driven to the other side of the base. It was a dreary, rainy day. Suddenly, the quilt covering them on the truck was pulled back. The sergeants yelled for everyone to get off the truck. All the recruits were grabbing their bags and other belongings, trying to hurry off the truck. The sergeants wanted everyone to stand on the line. No one knew where the line was because it was pouring down raining. "You have ten seconds to get up the steps," they were told. "Ready, go!" Everyone started running up the steps. All of the sudden the sergeant said, "Ten, seven, five, one, get down get, down get, down get, to the ground! Push the ground! Push the ground! Do push-ups!" Every time that they missed, they had to go back out there.

James was getting frustrated because he didn't understand. They told James to put his rucksack on his back. The drill sergeant would sit on his back as he started to do push-ups. James was trying to do push-ups, but he couldn't because there was a man sitting on his back. James continued, and the sergeant told everybody to toe line. The sergeant gave them twenty-five seconds to get up the steps. Mind you, they had to be on the third floor. Suddenly, they started counting again. "Twenty-five, fifteen, ten…" Everyone was running up the steps. James was so excited because he made it up to the steps and the barracks quickly. They all worked as a team with no one left behind. The sergeant yelled, "Get outside, get outside!" James was very frustrated. Everyone was outside in the pouring down rain doing push-ups.

James was regretting that day that and the decision that he had made. The sergeant said, "I will give you thirty seconds to get upstairs! And because everyone thought that thirty seconds was a long time, they all looked at each other, and they started pulling each other along. The countdown started, and everyone was rushing up the steps. This time, they all made it. The sergeants told the recruits, "Toe that line."

The first two weeks of basic training were the roughest times James had ever gone through. Even though he was in good shape, he had never run four and five miles before. He had never climbed a mountain before. He had never jumped out of a plane. He had never repelled out of a helicopter before. He was also learning to shoot his rifle. Each time he was done, he had to clean it. Even though James was a perfectionist, he had to learn new things in greater depth.

He missed home so badly, and he was always wondering how his mom was doing. So, he started writing his mom letters. He even wrote his mom five letters in one week. He kept wondering why she never wrote him back. Three weeks later James received one letter. He wondered why the dates were so far off. The sergeants told James that no one get letters for the first two weeks of training. They wanted the recruits at a certain emotional level. James continued to train. After that he had to go to the gas chamber, and he had to complete all the physical training tests. James did extremely well on his physical training tests. He ended up getting a patch. He did very well on shooting his weapon. He got all badges.

James called his mom on the sixth week and told her he was about to graduate. He told her what day the graduation was. James's family attended his graduation. When James looked at his sister, he noticed that she was a little big. He asked her, "What's wrong with you Karen? You look a little big?"

She said, "I'm pregnant."

James looked at her and said, "Wow." He didn't know what else to say.

James went on and went to his Advanced Individual training. He enjoyed that training. He'd never had any training like that before. It was so fun to him. The only thing that they knew how to do was have fun. The only thing James thought was, *Wow, this is a great relief.* Because the training was only for four weeks, he was wondering what he should do after the training. They told him he could either go home for a vacation or he could go straight to his permanent party.

James decided that he was going to go home to spend time with his mom and sister. He went over his sister's house to see what she was doing, and he enjoyed seeing her. Then he spent time with his mom. She went and showed him all over the city. She told everyone that her son was in the military. He was a member of the United States Army. His mom said, "I'm so proud of you I don't know what to do."

After that time, James went back to his permanent party. James had no idea what was about to happen to him. His life changed. James's mom told him don't forget to look for a church home. He said, "I plan to Mom." James started looking for a church home. He went down to the chapel, but he said, "No that's not enough. This is too quiet." James went asking around.

He went to another church, it was a Baptist church, and he felt that wasn't enough for him.

Then, he found a friend one night. He thought they were going out. Instead, the friend invited James to Friday night services. As he was sitting there, he was very curious about what kind of church it was. It was a non-denominational church, which he had never been to before. His friend said it was a Holiness Church. When James went to the church, he was used to devotion and other things like that. They had praise and worship, and suddenly they started worshipping God. James enjoyed it, and he wanted more.

James made sure he attended Bible study and prayer meetings. Every Sunday school, he was there because during this time James started getting more excited about God. When it was time for prayer, the pastor asked if anyone needed prayer. James was always up there, because he wanted more from God. He said, "Whatever I can get from Him, I want it. I don't care what it is I just want more from Him because I love Him." That's all James kept saying. No one accepted James. His friend that brought him was six foot seven inches and 236 pounds. He was tall, and light-skinned. It seemed like the whole church like him more. Every time his friend went up for prayer, they had a word for him. All the time. James would just sit there watch and say, "Lord, you don't have anything for me?" That's all he kept saying. He said, "Lord, you don't have anything for me?" Yet, he didn't get anything.

James continue to come, and one day something happened. There was a prayer meeting. They said they were going to have an all-night prayer meeting. James said, "I'm going because I want something from God. I'm going to pray; I'm going to keep praying until my change comes. I know God is going to tell me something." James had no idea what was about to happen in his life.

During this time, his military base had gone on alert. They were supposed to be going to Desert Storm. James was so afraid; he had no idea what was about to happen. He said to himself, "Man, am I about to die?" He said, "Lord, did you bring me all the way over here? I'm going to war?"

The night of the prayer meeting came. While he was sitting there praying, everyone else had their own partners. He stooped down on a chair—it was just him and God. And he started praying. During that time, James really knew how to pray. He had learned from listening to his father and listening to what his pastor said. The Lord had given him words to pray. When he started to pray, he shut his eyes, like a metallic click. As his eyes were shut, in the darkness, it seemed like a white quilt covered him, and it became light. From the top of his head to the soles of his feet works covered with light. This experience stretched him out on the floor as though he was on the cross.

He spoke with many tongues. Suddenly, he was out of his body, and he could see himself. He saw the pastor come over and put her hand on his stomach. There were many spiritual things happening in the service. God's Spirit was moving and there was healing and break-through happening all around.

The pastor told him that he was not going over to the war, for the war. "You're not going over there to fight. You're going over to see Him and to learn about Him. Your life will never be the same." That was the first word that the pastor had ever given to him. James didn't understand at that moment what had happened to him. He had an out-of-body experience looking at himself while speaking in tongues. He didn't tell anybody when it happened because he didn't know what to say.

James went to Saudi Arabia. He said goodbye to his mom and everyone who came over to see him off. He was so afraid. He had no idea what was about to occur. When he got to Saudi Arabia, he experienced the hottest weather he had ever been in. It was 136 degrees outside. In the shade it was 126 degrees. James needed to stay hydrated. They told him that everyone had to have one box of water. There were six waters in each box. Each soldier needed to drink six waters per day. Mind you, these are two liters of water. James wanted to keep his water cold, so he decided to dig a hole and put the water down in the hole and cover it. Everyone was looking at him, wondering why was he doing that? "This will keep the water cool," he said. He didn't like drinking hot water. The water was cooler. So, everyone else started doing the same thing. They finally reached a place where they could stay with air conditioning in each of the rooms.

The war in Iraq had already started where they were attacking Kuwait. James was so afraid because he didn't know was going to happen to them. He went back to his room, turned on his air, and began to read his Bible. James's mom had told him that whenever he was afraid, to open the Bible to Psalms 91. He started to read that. James laid down and prayed.

As he drifted off into sleep, in his room he kept hearing something in his room. He looked but didn't see anything. So, he turned back over, and as soon as he turned over, he heard something like a lion roaring. He heard the lion call him by name. "James! James! Be not afraid. I have chosen thee." James tried to turn over, but he could not move. The only thing that he could do was cry. The voice said, "James, James, be not afraid. I am Jesus." The only thing James knew to do was cry. Jesus told him that his cry was heard. "I see your desire and the love that you have for Me. And you will speak to many nations. And all that have rejected you, they have rejected Me. I will see you again. My servants will hear again. They will walk again. All that you believe, it shall be." Then He said, "Just believe."

During this time that Jesus speaking to James, He put him under a waterfall. Water was flowing over him, and on the bottom of his feet he was walking through the Bible, and the pages of the Bible were turning while filling him as Jesus spoke. James continued to listen to Him. God's presence was so strong, James couldn't stop crying and listening. He said to the Lord, "Lord, I love You with everything in me. And I will go wherever You want me to go. I'll say whatever You want me to say. I will die if it Your is will."

Jesus said, "I know. Since you were born, you were given the gift of love. It comes with a great deal of responsibility. And no one will accept you. Because what I have given you is unconditional. I need for you to give this to the world."

James said to Him, "I will, I will."

And the Lord said, "My son, every tear you have cried, I have it. Always remember this, even though man has rejected you, you are already accepted in heaven, and you will speak to many nations. You will speak to many kings. You will restore heavenly places to people who have no hope."

James said, "I want to make sure that I stay humble before You."

And Jesus said to him, "I know you will. The love that has been placed on the inside of you has increased so much." And he said, "I must go. I will come again when the time comes."

James cried out, "Wait!" But, Jesus disappeared.

James immediately turned over and was looking for Jesus but couldn't find Him. He looked all down the hallway and outside.

His friends kept asking him, "What's wrong? What's wrong? What happened?"

He said, "I can't explain it."

They said, "Tell me, man! What happened?"

James said, "The Lord appeared to me!"

They said, "What? We thought you were going to say something." They didn't believe him.

There was a guy that would always pick at his ears. While he was getting ready to hit James on the ear, James could see behind him. When he stepped into the shadow, he stepped back, and he changed his mind.

Chapter 6: Coming into Understanding

AS ALL THESE THINGS WERE HAPPENING TO James, he was coming into understanding why he was so rejected by man. Most of the time in his life, he had to understand that these things were happening because they rejected Jesus. Because James loved the Lord Jesus so much, he wanted so much from Him. When the Lord answered, James was always there. James said, "Lord, I will do work; Whatever You want me to do; I will go wherever You want me to go say whatever You want me to say." James meant everything in his heart because he loved the Lord. He loved the Lord with everything in him.

James began to listen to worship and praise songs all the time. He was laying on his bed, and there were other people in the room. He was sitting there with his eyes shut, and everyone else was taking a nap. As James was laying there, suddenly, he was worshiping praising

God. He had an out-of-body experience that pulled him out of his bed.

He went through the ceiling past the top of the earth past the stars. The Lord pulled him out there where everything was void. He showed him how it was in the beginning of time. As James came back down, he opened his eyes suddenly, and he was breathing hard and was looking around. The guy that was over across the room was still listening to music on his headphones. James was looking around as if something was wrong with him. But then he got up went to lunch, and as he was walking around, he noticed one thing. He could see differently, but he could also hear differently. What he started hearing and looking at things differently, James never experienced this before.

After he got done eating, he went off and kept working. He saw that there were someone having Bible study. James counseled them. One of the teachers said, "Hey, would you like to say something?" James was reading alone. So, he got up and spoke. When he spoke the words to them, everyone turned around. The people who were believers could not believe James was speaking the way he did. All of James's friends figured out why he was so quiet. Why he would just listenBut then when he got up and he spoke, the focus was on James. Something happened. James's best friend looked at him, and tears started rolling down his face. Later he said to James, "You are God's anointed." James didn't say anything. His friend said, "There was a glow behind you, a gold glow. That's the reason we were looking at you the way we were. And it got brighter. The Lord is with you James." And James didn't say anything.

He continue to do the things that he was doing and stay humble before the Lord. People were trying to understand how he learned the Word the way that he did. It was so fluid, and he had so much power and understanding. Many of the people were amazed that God was advancing him so fast in the things of God. Some people were actually confused at how he rapidly he was maturing in his walk with God. It normally took people decades to arrive in the place where God had taken him in relatively short time.

He went to church services that they had at the chapel on base. The clergyman that was there looked over at him. I didn't know that minister at all. And he asked James, "Would you like to speak?" James was astonished because he had no desire to speak. He was just there listening. But, he got up and spoke to each one of them there.

There was one guy that was sitting there and would not look up. James asked him, What's troubling your heart?"

And the guy said, "I can't look at you. It says if you're looking right at me, I can't lie."

James was astonished. He said to the man, "You don't have to be ashamed of anything. The Lord will forgive you of all your sins." And so, when James went back to his room, he prayed to God for greater understanding. He didn't want to get beside himself. He always told the Lord that he wanted to stay humble before Him. So, as James was praying, he drifted off into a dream.

In the dream, he was on the beach with his friends. His friends walked away from him and said they wanted to go inside. But James wanted to stay on the beach while watching the water hit the shore. Suddenly, a man walked up to him he asked him, "Will you walk with me?"

And James said, "Sure, I don't have anything else to do."

The men asked, "Why are you so discouraged?"

James told him, "No one understands me.

The man that was walking with him said, "No one understands me either. I know how you feel."

James stumbled, and the man grabbed James's hand so that he would not fall. And James told him, "Oh, thank you." During this time, James never looked up at the man. Suddenly, they started walking up a sandy hill. James began stumbling as the hill became rock. And as they were walking, James almost fell again. Suddenly, the man picked James up and carried him. the continued to walk up the hill as the hill got steeper and steeper, and suddenly, the man took one big step. James never looked up at the man because he was too busy down to see what was under him. When the man took a step, he stepped over a mountain, and then he stepped over another mountain. He was talking to James, and he was telling him all about the world and the many places that he was see.

And the man said to James, "Many people have rejected me, so they will reject you." Then, all of a sudden, James was on the other side of the hill, but as they were walking down the hill, James said, "This side is so peaceful. No one's there."

And the man said to him, "What do you mean?"

James said, "It's like no one has been on the beach at all."

The man said, "That's because the water has washed the feet of people." He walked a bit further with James, and then he put them down. They kept walking on the beach. And all of a sudden, James heard his friends call him, but he ignored his friends.

The man said to James, "I must go. I must go and see my father.

James said, "Oh, I understand."

The man said, "Don't worry. I will always be with you."

And James said, "Huh? What do you mean, you'll always be with me?"

Then, he heard his friends call him again. As James turned his head to look at his friends, the man let go of his hands. James looked back because he was looking for him, and when he looked up, he saw the man was ascending to heaven.

James yelled, "Please don't leave me!"

He said, "I will always be with you."

James shouted again, "Please come back! Don't leave me!"

As James cried, the man said, "I will always be with you."

James cried, "Please, come back!"

And the man said, "Always be with you."

Suddenly, James recognized the man. He said, "I didn't know."

And Jesus said, "I will always be with you," and He disappeared out of sight.

And James said, "Forgive me for not knowing who You were."

James woke up in tears. Things had changed. During this time, while he was going through the war, he began to minister to people. Not only was he ministering to people, but people were getting and filled with the Holy Ghost. James and his friends continued to minister. That's when the war intensified. Many of the soldiers were frightened to face real combat but James and his friend were not afraid. The Holy Spirit had given him a great sense of peace.

And when he went to sleep, he feared nothing. A lot of chaos was going on during that time. And at that time, every time James spoke to someone, their life was free, even his friend who had brought him to the church for the first time, God has touched his life. How many people were saved?

When the war, was over, it was time to go back home. During that time, there were things that happened while

James was on the plane. They flew over the United States for the first time. James had a very sick feeling in the pit of his stomach, like he was going into land of sickness, and he did not like that feeling. So, James ignored that feeling.

And when he went back to that church once he landed, it was as if he did not need that church anymore. So, he started looking for a different church. James said that the church he went to was not enough for him. James and his friend went to find a different church, an Apostolic Church. This time James and his friends started looking and listening to the ways of the apostolic, walking the apostolic way. James already knew about the Kingdom of God and that God was calling him into the ministry of an apostle. God calling was so strong on his life that almost everyone who came across him knew God's hand was on his life. James continued to stay humble as God continued to use him.

There were a lot of people arguing over the Bible at church. There was one young lady who was there, and she kept getting upset in such a way that she ended up getting sick because James told her to stop arguing over the Bible. And he told the other woman she had been arguing with that she would suffer the same fate as the first young lady. The young lady got so upset because she had a bad temper and she wanted to be right because she was so much denied. James said to her, "You're not denied; you're accepted by heaven, so don't fret." But, she didn't listen to him. All of a sudden, she broke out with sores from the top of her head to the bottom of her feet. The sickness was so bad she had to be sent to Germany, and she didn't get to come back to the United States. So, at that time, her husband told James what happened, and James talked to her on the phone. James said to her, "What have you learned?"

She said to him, "Please forgive me."

"Sins are forgiven," he told her, "you are restored."

There, doctors were stumped because they were trying to figure out what the source of the illness was. But, all of a sudden, the sores thesaurus went completely away. Even where they had pulled up the skin, it was as if there was nothing there. So, for a few more days, they kept doing tests. And then after that, they sent her home. The lady was so excited because she saw the change that was about to happen in her life.

Chapter 7: Walking in the Work

AS TIME WENT ON, JAMES STARTED GETTING used to being back in the United States of America. James enjoyed being with his friends who were saved and had a converted life. James taught them the things that they needed to know. He taught them the things that he had learned when he was over in the desert.

James started to have many different experiences. One day, James went to see his mother, because it had been a very long time since he had seen her. When James walked in, she looked at him surprise. She said, "James, it's as though I don't know you. When I look at you, I can tell that you have changed."

James did not say anything. He just stared at his mother Martha. James finally said, "Mom, I missed you."

Martha said, "I thought I was going to have to send the National Guard out to find you, even though you're in the army." They laughed.

He told his mother, "During that time, we were not allowed to call home."

So, when the next day came, the city had a parade for James. They also had a banquet for James. As James was walking downtown with his mom, James saw a blind man who was sitting on the side of the road. The man was asking for food.

Martha said, "James leave the man alone."

And James said, "No." James sent his mom on into the store to get something to eat. As James walked up to the man, he asked him, "What can I do for you?"

The blind man told him, "I just want something to eat."

James replied, "For me to get you something to eat, I need you to do something for me."

The blind man responded by saying, "What is this about?"

James said, "I know that you can't see, but I need you to do something for me. To go get something for you to eat, something greater." So, the man told James that he would do it. James told him, "I'm going right into the store, and I'm going to get you something to eat, but I want you to keep your eyes shut." James went into Subway, purchased a meal for the homeless man, and he brought it back out to him. James said, "I need for you to keep your eyes shut. I'm going to put this right in your lap."

The man asked him, "When shall I open my eyes?

James said, "When it's time." As James looked at the man, he said, "Lord bless him, and keep him, and restore him."

As the man sat there with the food in his lap, James walked away from him, When James got to the end of the corner, the man opened his eyes, and at that moment he opened his eyes, everyone turned around because they heard him screaming. "I can see! I can see! I can see! Hallelujah!" The man dropped his food on the ground because he was so excited that he could see for the first time in his life. The man started saying, "It was a man. There was a man. I can see!" People were just looking at him in shock. James turned around and looked once before he kept going on with his mom.

As James walked home, his mom was talking to him. She said, "James, I noticed that your spirit is so humble." The soul astonishes, for the first time in her life about her son didn't even know what to say. She said, "I'm filled with joy!"

James said, "Oh, Mom, can I ask you a question?"

And she said, "Yes James."

"Why didn't you tell me?"

Martha asked, "Why didn't I tell you what?"

"That I was chosen," said James.

Martha said, "Baby, I knew that you were chosen when you were inside of me. When I would read the Word to you, you would be ever so still. Then Martha asked James, "What are your plans?"

And James said, "To do God's will. That's the only thing that I desire." So, Martha remained quiet. She did not speak a word.

As time went on, James went back to his base. And he was talking to many people; so many people from that time on, wanted to have Bible study with him. But then, time it was almost time for him to leave. And he made a lot of friends who were saved and renewed, and people were being held. The way that James did things was in secret. No one knew what was going on with these miracles. James was happy.

One of the subjects James was teaching on was restoration. James also was teaching on how your past can affect your present and future. He told his story of how everyone turned away from him. No one accepted him; he was either too short, or too small, or he wasn't like everyone else. James told everyone, "When you see that things are happening in your life, even though you're rejected by men, you'll always be accepted by God. And that's the greatest acceptance there is." James told them this, to learn God is oh, and to learn of his love god's love no. The world has a love that is conditional. What you get from them is based on what you do for them. And if you don't do anything for them, you won't get anything from them. So, it's a love that's always conditional. God loves regardless, because he is love. The Greatest Love of all.

So, James went on and talked and discovered there were many that were broken on the inside. James a skin store very, very wide. But, there was one thing that James yearned for. He had God's love, but he wanted a partner. As hard as he tried to find someone, he couldn't find that person for him. Every time he was with someone, and she did something, he already knew it was going to happen.

He remembered when he was dating one young lady, she asked if she could use his car. James, with his giving heart, went ahead and let her use the car. But, she had an alternative motive. She went out with another man in James's car, while James was sitting at home. He knew what she was going to do, and when James told her about it, she got upset because she thought that James had someone following her. But he didn't. She had no idea who she was talking to though. As time went on, James decided to go ahead and do God's will, knowing that when the time came, He would send him that special person. He said, "Lord, I want them to understand me as I understand you." If someone walked up to James and told him this, have the same as mind the love God as you love God. Because it will be a struggle for her because of the gift of love that you have on the inside of you. James remembered he recognize what she was saying because we have been told this a long time ago. Visitation.

James continued on, and the only thing he did was serve God, speak to people, and restore people. People were getting saved and filled with the Holy Ghost. And, there were many followers. Who were really wondering this church? He told them, "The church is on the inside of you. So, this that I give you, I want you to go out, and I want you to give it to someone else. Help someone else's life be restored."

James's life was always busy, and because people call all the time during the day, James was growing tired. He could not get any rest. One night, James decided that he was going to turn his phone off and just have a deep sleep.. After he turned his phone on the next morning, he noticed that his voicemail was so full. People were calling as soon as he woke up. They couldn't understand why they couldn't reach him. The voicemail was full.

James told each person he spoke to, "I just needed some rest."

They all laughed and said something such as, "Please forgive me. You've talked about so much, you have spoiled me. And you turned your phone off, so I couldn't talk to you."

James laughed, and he his life. James's life was such a beauty to the world. James said, "I wish the world could see the love of God the way that I could see it. I wish that everyone could see the love the way they do during Christmas time. When they have the love of giving and everyone is celebrating Christ. I wish that we could do this every day." When James celebrated Christmas, he really, really celebrated Christmas. He told everyone that he enjoyed Christmas more than his birthday. And they would ask him why. He would always say, "Because it's my Savior's birthday. My Savior who chose me to touch and bring His people home.

This is where a shift took place in James's life, and he began to embrace the calling and purpose of the Lord Jesus Christ in His life. The destiny of the Apostle Paul was eternally shifted when *he* encountered the Lord Jesus Christ on the road to Damascus. James's life was also totally remade after receiving the vision of Jesus Christ.

Chapter 8: Following the Vision of Jesus Christ

NOW THAT JAMES COULD SEE WHAT WAS going on, he understood the reasons why Jesus chose him to do His work and His will. James set out to follow the vision that Jesus had given him. Even as a child, James understood that he was rejected, and he was pushed to the side. As James grew up, things were happening to him. Everyone who James talked to would not accept him. He could not understand while he was growing up why these things were occurring. The one thing James could see about his childhood was that if these things had not happened to him, he would not have had a testimony to give to the people and could restore them.

James could quickly identify with those who were broken. James would see people in his ministry who were going the wrong way. They would breakout and go into ministry with brokenness. They would transfer that spirit to the next person that was already broken. So, James set out to speak to the leaders, and talk to them, and let them know that Jesus loves them first. James said that, "No matter what it takes, I'm going to touch God's people and bring them back to Him because I gave Him my word." Even then, James was not accepted, but it didn't bother him because he loved Jesus so much that nothing could move him. No matter what obstacle came his way, he kept pressing forward.

When James spoke the Word to people, it didn't matter who you were, you would be restored. James would encounter many ministries that were big but battered in Christ. James would get phone calls from other churches to come and speak with the people to help them to restore the people. James would tell the people, from the leaders, the bishops, the apostles, the prophet, to the pastor that, "First, we have to restore the head. If you can't restore the head, the whole body will die." Once they had the leadership meetings, where they would talk and pray together, James would say, "Let me give you this one scripture that goes with restoration. In the book of 2 Chronicles 7:14, God says, 'If my people who are called by My name would humble themselves and pray, seek My face turn from their wicked ways, and then I will hear from Heaven. I will forgive their sins and heal their lands…'"

He would tell them, "First, we must repent, and humble ourselves before the presence of God. Most people come to God with a 'just asking for something' attitude. They don't know how to surrender. That person ends up going back into the same thing that they just got rid of. It's like when you give your life to Christ for the first time; you're surrendering everything that has occurred in your life. You're laying it at the cross." James said to them, "Jesus died on the cross that we might be free. He died on the cross, that we may be able to come to Him."

James was so passionate about it, that every time he spoke, he drew people to him. When James came into different ministries, the people would draw close to him and would turn away from their pastors. They would turn away from their bishops. They would turn away from their apostles. The men and women of God would get upset with James, saying, "You're taking away my people."

James responded by saying, "These people don't belong to any of us. They belong to God. I'm not taking anything from you. The only thing I'm doing is giving what God has given to me, to give to them. Please, understand that I came in here to do my Father's will, and you invited me too," James said. "The people are thirsty for water. They are hungry for food. They're burning for God's will. They need the love of Christ in their lives because they have been battered, bruised, and rejected."

As James spoke to the clergy, he told them that he understood them because they have been rejected just like he was rejected. "That's the reason why He called me to tell you to come to this place, to help you to restore His people." James told them not to give up, because He loved them, and He was going to stay right there with them, regardless of the circumstances. James told them, "The Bible says to be in the world, not of the world. As men and women of God, we have to separate ourselves from the world because we are trying to blend in with the world and God's will. That's the trick of the enemy. The enemy is tricking us, causing us to sabotage souls because we're blending in with the world. We wonder why we can't keep them. We're not the authenticity of what God has said. We come up with excuses, but the Bible says that we are without excuse. We keep saying that we all fall short of the glory of God, but we keep using excuses. We are not willing to repent and admit that we have done wrong and are lost. The only thing we have to do is come back to the remembrance of our beginning. Once we get to our beginning, we become new again. Pouring out all of the old things, and all things become new."

As they heard James speaking, they became excited. They repented themselves. They heard him. One of the things he said in the beginning was, "He who has an ear, let him hear what the Spirit of the Lord is saying to the church. Your soul, so the change can come. Be set free from the bondage and the trickery that the world has given you. Jesus love you."

James told them that whatever he had to do to help them to get to the finish line, he was going to do it. He did not care how much time it took to accomplish the goal. He was dedicated to helping them complete it. James wanted it done. James kept saying to the Lord that he needed so much help. "There are so many people in the world that are battered. There are so many people that are bruised and put down. They're rejected and calling out Your name."

The Lord then spoke to James, and said, "Go and find Me the biggest building. I will show you. Put your hands on it. Lay your hands on this building, and I will give this building to you."

James searched for many years trying to find the right building. One day, he drove up to that building. He laid his hands on that building. God told him that He was going to give that building to him. James was waiting on God to give him that building while he continued to work on restoring souls. With the passion and the love he had in his heart, he wants everyone to feel the love of Christ as he felt it. He told everyone about the testimony about when he first met Him. He said, "I wish you could see as I see."

One bishop asked James, "How do you see?"

James answered and said, "Honestly, I can't see as everyone anymore." He said, "I even tried glasses, and I still can't see as everyone else sees."

"I don't understand what you mean," said the bishop.

James said that when he saw the Lord, He changed his eyesight. "I don't see the flesh; I see the heart. I'm on a mission until death to gather God's people. Not only in the United States, but through the whole world. I must show everyone that God is love. He is love, and He has not forgotten us."

So many people try to love in so many ways. If they would first learn to love Christ, even the divorce rates would be lower. There would not be as much violence in the world, if they would first learn the love of Christ. James said that his heart hurts every night when he prays and thinks of how many people are lost. He said his heart hurts when he sees people on the side of the road hungry and thirsty; they need food. They are homeless and hopeless. He said his heart hurts when he walks through the store, feeling the people and knowing the only thing they need is just love. His heart hurts from the deception presented by the church, where the people don't even want to attend anymore because of how the church has done them. James told them that when they come to church, they should not to look at the person. They should listen to the Word that God is saying.

Chapter:9 Understanding the Vision

THIS TESTIMONY ABOUT THE LIFE OF JAMES IS both powerful and true. The reason that I can share this story with such insight and clarity is because this is my story. The Holy Spirit inspired me years ago to write this work and share the power of His healing and reconciliation. I have shared the previous chapters of this story from the perspective of an eye-witness. As I close this book, I want to share my heart and how God brought me understanding and healing.

As James started to look back over his life, he reflected on the why and the how and the where.

Every other thing had been filled in. He understood why the Lord choose him to do this work.

So, James wrote the vision that God gave him down and made it plain so that everyone that he spoke to could understand.

They wouldn't be confused about it or need to ask questions about it.

The only thing that they would need to do when it came to their life is to make a decision about what they were going to do once they find out that their past has affected their present. If they didn't do anything about it, it would impact their future.

James spoke like this, "In my findings of Jesus Christ, I always asked the question of, why? Why did He choose me? I know that in my life, I have been rejected by many, but I was accepted by Him, and He is the greatest Love of *all*."

***

We are all born into this world with innocence as a baby. If we could just illustrate, and not forget, that innocence and humbleness we had as a child, the reembrace would make us better people. As we grow up and become adults, we start thinking on our own, and we feel that we can do whatever we want. Because God gave us the ability to choose in the Garden of Eden, we have a choice to do His will. When it comes to love, it is unconditional if you get it from Jesus Christ. Love requires quite a bit of sacrifice.

When it comes to love, people will come to you with all types of love. They will tell you, if you love me, then I'll do this for you. But, when it comes to Jesus, when you love Him, He will love you unconditionally.

You won't need to do anything but just love. The Lord Jesus Christ said in John 14:15, "If you love me, you will keep my Commandments." God loved us so much that He gave His only begotten Son. So, when you think about how much He loves us, what man would lay down his life for a friend? The more that you put into God, the more you get out of Him. Some people only put a little into Him, and they only get a little out of Him because they don't have "time." They only have time for what they want.

When it comes to the love of God, what I have found was that He is the greatest love of all. Because He loved me so much, He gave me so many things, and I would rather have spiritual things than natural things any day of my life.

When it comes to my life and me and my house, we serve the Lord in love. We give to people in love. No matter what it is, we give in love. I know there were times when I was persecuted because I love so much, and I love so deep.

I know that love is so deep that you cannot understand how far it can go. Think about how an eagle can fly to the highest height of the sky and get to the edge of the earth. He's able to see out into space. I think about how there is thin air up there.

When one considers the sea and how deep it is, there is also thin air down there. Love is the same thing. Love is thin air.

There are only a few that want the love of God. To love Him, comes at a price. There are things that one has to give up. Loving God is hard when one mixes personal desires with the pursuit of loving God.

I've learned that through God's love, all things are possible. If you believe the love of Christ is inside of you, nothing is impossible. You can reach the highest heights in life. Through His love and believing by faith, all things are possible. No matter what it is. It doesn't matter if someone is handicapped. It doesn't matter if someone is sick. It doesn't matter what their situation is. All things are possible through Christ. Because of His love, He died on the cross for us.

Even while He was dying on the cross, there was still healing going on. We should think of how much someone could love us, to still be healing us, while dying on a rugged cross. Never forget what He has done for us and what we should be doing every day of our lives.

We should rededicate our lives and think back to when we were children. When we didn't know evil. We would just play in the sand box with our friends. For example, if a child pushed us, we would not be friends for a moment, but we would forgive and come back to play again.

We should continue to love and forgive. If we look in our past at all of the heart breaks and disappointments with all of the things that have stopped life, we can start to blame. This is where bitterness sets in, and it becomes a roadblock. As you grow, that pain grows like a weed on the inside of you. You become more and more bitter. Then, when you really try to love, it's hard because you lose the favor of the of the love Christ birthed in you when you were born. Once you find out that the thing deep on the inside of you is saying, "I'm trying to get there. I'm trying to love," you just have to surrender.

It's written in 2nd Chronicles 7:14 , "If My people who are called by my name would humble themselves and pray, seek My face, and turn from their wicked ways." God said, "Then I will hear from heaven, I will forgive their sins, and heal their lands." God wants us to humble ourselves as little children because we are His children. When we humble ourselves as little children, we can hear from Him. We can obey Him because we love Him. I remember when I was growing up, and I used to get in trouble with my mom and dad. I remember that even though I might have gotten in trouble, I knew that my mom and dad loved me. Because they loved me so much, it pushes me eve today to give out the love that I had.

When Christ came to me and gave me the gift of love, the only thing that is on the inside of me. Through life and death, I want to give this love. I'm not holding any bitterness on the inside, because no matter what someone does to me and no matter what someone says to me to hurt me, I still love them. The only thing I say when people hurt me is, "Lord, forgive them. For they know not what they do." What they don't understand is that when they persecute me, the only thing I give them back is *love*. Amen.

Lightning Source UK Ltd.
Milton Keynes UK
UKHW010634200420
361986UK00001B/13